Becoming a Haiku Poet

Becoming a Haiku Poet

~

Michael Dylan Welch

PRESS HERE
Sammamish, Washington

PRESS HERE
22230 NE 28th Place
Sammamish, Washington
98074-6408 USA

ISBN 978-1-878798-36-7

First printing, September 2015

The essay in this book was first published on Gary Warner's
"Haiku World" website in April of 2003. It has since been published on
numerous other websites, including the author's own Graceguts.com
website, and has been translated into several different languages.

Poems by Mark Brooks, Jerry Kilbride, Peggy Willis Lyles, Ebba Story,
and Paul O. Williams are reprinted by permission of each poet.

Design, typography, and photography by Michael Dylan Welch.

Essay text set in 14/24 Garamond Premier Pro,
with headings set in 22/24 Eras Bold ITC.

www.graceguts.com
www.nahaiwrimo.com

Contents

Foreword 7

Becoming a Haiku Poet 9

Haiku Checklist. 21

Next Steps 25

Resources. 27

Foreword

At the beginning of the haiku journey, few people set out with the intention of becoming a haiku poet. It mostly starts with a curiosity, fascination, if not infatuation for these tiny poems. The unknown can be unnerving, but the desire to learn drives any budding poet forward. Having taught haiku, I've watched students devour them through reading and class discussion, then stumble once asked to write. The questions come flooding in: Do syllables matter? What's the structure? What all goes into a haiku? There's a semester to help them figure out the answers. However, most students don't learn about haiku through the traditional classroom.

Fortunately, the real secret to becoming a haiku poet is to start writing haiku. Read, write, immerse yourself in the haiku community. This handbook, written by a poet who has spent most of his life journeying with haiku, provides the basic tools in a careful balance of practical craft tips and cultural background to properly get you started.

AUBRIE COX

Becoming a Haiku Poet

"Haiku has this rather fantasmagorical property: that we always suppose we ourselves can write such things easily."

—ROLAND BARTHES, *Empire of Signs*

When I first tried writing haiku, my attempts were based on very limited information. The quality and effectiveness was poor as a result. My school teachers meant well, but often presented only a superficial and sometimes misguided notion of haiku. If you're new to haiku, you may be in the same situation—without knowing it. While too much information can also impede the poetic impulse, with haiku, as with other genres of poetry, it's worthwhile to move beyond superficialities to gain a more substantial knowledge of the genre. So what is haiku, and how does one become a haiku poet?

The most important characteristic of haiku is how it conveys, through implication and suggestion, a moment of keen perception and perhaps insight into nature or human nature. Haiku does not *state* this insight, however, but implies it. In the last hundred years—in Japanese and English-language haiku—implication has been achieved most successfully through the use of objective imagery and ju. This means you avoid words that interpret what you experience, such as saying something is "beautiful" or "mysterious," and rely on words that objectively convey the facts of what you see, hear, smell, taste, and touch. Instead of writing about your *reactions* to stimuli, in a good haiku you write about those things that *cause* your reactions. If you remember nothing else about crafting haiku, remember that. If your haiku take advantage of this technique, your readers can experience the same feelings you felt, without your having to explain them.

spring breeze—

the pull of her hand

as we near the pet store

—*Michael Dylan Welch*

A haiku also centers structurally on a pause or caesura ("kire" in Japanese). By juxtaposing two elements or parts (with one of the elements spanning over two of the poem's three lines), the two parts create a spark of energy, like the gap in a spark plug. The two elements of a good haiku may seem unrelated at first glance, but if the reader lingers on them sufficiently, he or she may notice a reverberation. When you realize the connection between the two parts (sometimes called an "internal comparison"), you have a "spark" of realization, an "aha" moment. As a writer of haiku, it's your job to allow the poem to have that spark—and not to spell it out for the reader. This is perhaps the most difficult thing to do with haiku, as well as its most important—yet often least understood—structural characteristic.

> new moon . . .
> curve of the steeple bell
> in winter twilight
> —*Ebba Story*

Another key strategy in haiku is the seasonal reference. Traditional Japanese haiku use a season word ("kigo") to anchor the poem in time and to allude to other poems that use the same reference. While a formalized set of season words has yet to fully evolve in English-language haiku, many seasonal references are intuitive, and are worth including in your haiku. A simple example would be "snow" to indicate winter, or "frog" to indicate spring. You could name the season also, but the best season words are more subtle than that. Some terms can be troublesome, as in "dry grass," which may mean winter in some places (such as in New Jersey) but summer in other places (such as California). As you begin to learn haiku that are well known in English, you will be able to allude to or understand allusions to other haiku (including Japanese haiku). It's important, with season words, to usually use just one in each haiku (unless one clearly dominates another). As you become more experienced with haiku, you'll discover that words often have seasonal associations to them that you might not have been conscious of before. You can maximize the effect of these words by using them carefully in your haiku.

> Mother's scarf
> slides from my shoulder—
> wild violets
> —*Peggy Willis Lyles*

Speaking of writing carefully, haiku is often thought of as the most compressed poem in the world. This doesn't just mean it's the briefest, but that it packs a lot more into its scant three lines than you might have in other poems or prose. This is thanks to the techniques I've already described. With objectivity, the images reverberate for themselves, opening up for the reader rather than being closed down by the use of subjective explanation. With a caesura, you create energy through the juxtaposition between the two elements, which may be a background or context, juxtaposed with a foreground or focus. And with a season word, you connect the poem to nature and time and other poetry. Above all, a haiku mysteriously creates an emotional impression, a whole that is often much greater than the sum of its parts.

      gone from the woods
      the bird I knew
      by song alone
              —Paul O. Williams

On a practical note, haiku never have titles, almost never rhyme, and seldom use overt metaphor and simile. The reasoning for this is that these devices often make the reader more aware of the words than their meaning. Haiku, as Jack Kerouac once said, should be as simple as porridge. Use direct and simple language. Avoid long, conceptual, Latinate words. And note, too, that the word "haiku" is both singular and plural (thus one doesn't say "haikus," even though Kerouac did to rhyme with "blues").

> withering wind
> the fence-builder pulls a nail
> from his lips
> —*Mark Brooks*

You may have noticed that thus far I've said almost nothing about form in haiku. That's because form is not nearly as important as the other strategies I've covered. Form, in fact, is the most misunderstood aspect of haiku. Haiku is frequently mistaught in schools, and many textbooks and dictionary definitions are superficial and sometimes even misguided. Many textbooks are simply out of date, and haiku is best understood as a genre of poetry, not a form. Haiku in Japan are arranged in a single vertical line, and *traditionally* (meaning, not always) have three parts of 5, 7, and then 5 Japanese sound symbols (which are not the same as syllables). Many English-language textbooks say that haiku in English should be 5-7-5 syllables. This assertion exhibits a gross misunderstanding of the differences between Japanese and English syllables and how the languages differ (for example, the word "haiku" itself is two syllables in English, but counts as *three* sounds in Japanese). Indeed, the vast bulk of literary haiku written in English are usually shorter than seventeen syllables, and their authors choose to follow or apply a free or organic form rather than an arbitrary external syllable count that hasn't proved effective or appropriate in the English language. This fact may come as a surprise to many poets who are new to haiku (or even some who think they aren't that new to it), but it's worth reviewing books such as Cor van den Heuvel's *The Haiku Anthology* (Norton, third edition, 1999), Jim Kacian's *Haiku in English: The First Hundred Years* (Norton, 2013), and William J. Higginson's *The Haiku Handbook* (Kodansha, 25th anniversary edition, 2010) to see examples and to understand why haiku in English is best written without a slavish adherence to a set syllabic form.

mime
lifting
fog

—Jerry Kilbride

When you write your haiku, focus on perceptions and images. Be aware of the seasons and what you perceive through your five senses. Write about your perceptions objectively. Strive to master the understanding of what is objective and subjective in what you write. Learn the difference between description and inference, so your poem can avoid doing any inferring for the reader; instead, let the reader infer ideas and connections from the carefully juxtaposed objective descriptions you present. With this focus, relying on the perceptions you receive through your five senses, and using the technique of juxtaposition, your haiku can be excellent. They will be far more effective than the pseudo-haiku that parade around email in-boxes making light of some subject or another—or lots of other pseudo-haiku that the writers don't even realize is not really haiku. With the proper haiku fundamentals in mind, you can write haiku that rise above the superficial under-standings that are commonly presented or believed about haiku. Using the more advanced techniques, which you can learn the basics of quickly, but which can take a lifetime to master, you can write effective haiku. It isn't hard to write haiku that are far more successful than what fits the popular misperception of haiku merely as a 5-7-5 poem. Too often those poems lack many of the other techniques that are more vital to haiku than a superficial external structure. Search for the deeper form of haiku—the keen perceptions that are presented objectively through the use of juxtaposition. Read many good haiku to see what makes them work. Observe life around you closely and see freshly and authentically so that you may imply life's daily epiphanies effectively. Let the "aha" moments of life be implied by your carefully chosen words describing nature and human nature. Then you, too, will become a haiku poet.

> meteor shower . . .
> a gentle wave
> wets our sandals
> —*Michael Dylan Welch*

Haiku Checklist

"If one really wishes to be master of an art, technical knowledge of it is not enough. One has to transcend technique so that the art becomes an 'artless art' growing out of the Unconscious."
—D. T. Suzuki, in his introduction to
Eugen Herrigel's *Zen in the Art of Archery*

For haiku inspiration, look closely at everything around you in nature, at home, at school, or at work. Write your haiku first, letting yourself be free and creative. Then ask the following questions about your haiku to help you improve them. Think of these not as rules for haiku, but targets—not every haiku will hit every target.

1. How long is your haiku? It's usually good to write in three lines of about ten to seventeen syllables. In English, haiku don't have to be in the pattern of 5-7-5 syllables—the following questions are much more important.

2. Does your haiku name or suggest one of the seasons—spring, summer, fall, or winter? In Japanese, a *kigo* or "season word" tells readers when the poem happens, such as saying "tulips" for spring or "snow" for winter. This is one of the most important things to do in haiku.

3. Does your poem make a "leap," by having two parts? In Japanese, a *kireji* or "cutting word" usually cuts the poem into two parts. Giving your poem two distinct parts (never three), both grammatically and imagistically, is also one of the most important things to do in haiku. It's not enough to juxtapose two images; they must also have some chemistry between them, creating what I like to call a "juxtapop."

4. Is your haiku about common, everyday events in nature or human life? To help you with this target, describe what you experience through your five senses.

5. Does your poem give readers a feeling? It can do this by presenting what *caused* your feeling rather than the feeling itself. So others can feel what you felt, don't explain or judge what you describe.

6. Is your poem in the present tense? To make your haiku feel like it's happening right now, use the present tense.

7. Did you write from your own personal experience? When you write other kinds of poetry, you can make things up, but try not to do that with haiku, at least not often. Memories are okay, though.

8. How did you capitalize or punctuate your poem? Haiku are usually not sentences (they're often fragments), so they don't need to start with a capital, or end with a period.

9. Does your haiku avoid a title and rhyme? Haiku are not like other poems, which may have these things. Haiku don't have titles and rarely rhyme.

10. What can you do with your haiku? Can you illustrate them, pair them with photographs, collect them in a notebook, or display them? Can you write haiku in your journal every day, enter them in a contest, publish them, or share them at a poetry reading?

With practice, you won't need to ask yourself these questions about your haiku (that's what Bashō meant when he said to "learn the rules and then forget them"). Enjoy noticing life more closely through your five senses!

> *Don't write about your emotions in haiku.*
> *Instead, write about what caused your emotions.*

Next Steps

"Haiku should be as simple as porridge."
—JACK KEROUAC, *The Dharma Bums*

1. Buy a pocket notebook and keep it with you.
2. Write haiku as often as possible, or at least make notes to develop into haiku later. Record what you experience through your five senses.
3. Read books of Japanese haiku in translation, and books of and about haiku in English.
4. Join or start a local haiku group.
5. Join a national haiku organization, such as the Haiku Society of America or Haiku Canada.
6. Subscribe to a few printed haiku journals, and read online haiku journals.
7. Get involved with a Facebook haiku group, such as NaHaiWriMo (National Haiku Writing Month, which has daily writing prompts year-round, although February is the "official" month).
8. Expand your interest in haiku to explore senryu, haibun, haiga, renku, rengay, and tanka.
9. Set yourself a goal to write 100, 200, or 500 haiku (be patient with yourself), and then try sending the best out for publication.
10. Teach or inspire others to write haiku.

Resources

Please search online for the following selected haiku resources. Also search for corresponding Facebook and Twitter sites. See also the author's website at Graceguts.com.

Haiku Organizations

American Haiku Archives
Association Francophone de Haiku
Australia Haiku Society
British Haiku Society
Deutsche Haiku Gesellschaft
Haiku Canada
The Haiku Foundation
Haiku International Association
Haiku New Zealand
Haiku North America
Haiku Society of America
L'Associazione Italiana Haiku
NaHaiWriMo (National Haiku Writing Month)
World Haiku Association

Many other countries outside Japan have active haiku organizations, including Belgium, Brazil, Bulgaria, Columbia, Croatia, the Czech Republic, Denmark, Holland, Hungary, India, Ireland, Lithuania, Poland, Romania, Russia, Serbia, Slovenia, Sweden, and Turkey. For tanka resources, search online for the Tanka Society of America and Tanka Canada.

Haiku Books

The Art of Haiku, Stephen Addiss
Haiku: Asian Arts & Crafts for Creative Kids, Patricia Donegan
Haiku: A Poet's Guide, Lee Gurga
The Haiku Handbook, William J. Higginson
Haiku in English: The First Hundred Years, Jim Kacian,
Philip Roland, and Allan Burns, editors
The Haiku Anthology, Cor van den Heuvel, editor

Also read translations by Stephen Addiss, R. H. Blyth, Donald Keene, Hiroaki Sato, Haruo Shirane, Makoto Ueda, and Burton Watson, especially biographies and translations of Japanese masters such as Bashō, Buson, Chiyo-ni, Issa, Santōka, and Shiki.

Haiku Publishers

Bottle Rockets Press	King's Road Press
Brooks Books	Press Here
Deep North Press	Red Moon Press
Iron Press	Snapshot Press

Haiku Journals

Acorn	*Mariposa*
Bones	*Mayfly*
Blithe Spirit	*Modern Haiku*
Bottle Rockets	*Paper Wasp*
Frogpond	*Presence*
Haiku Canada Review	*South by Southeast*
The Heron's Nest	*Tinywords*
A Hundred Gourds	*Upstate Dim Sum*

Made in the USA
San Bernardino, CA
27 June 2016